DATE			

TO RENEW THIS BOOK
CALL 275-5367

© THE BAKER & TAYLOR CO.

WHY WE LIVE WITH ANIMALS

Why We Live with Animals

POEMS BY ALVIN GREENBERG

COFFEE HOUSE PRESS :: MINNEAPOLIS :: 1990

Cover and interior wood engravings by Gaylord Schanilec

Back cover photo by Greg Helgeson

The publisher thanks the following organizations whose sup-
port helped make this book possible: The National Endowment
for the Arts, a federal agency; Dayton Hudson Foundation;
Cowles Media/Star Tribune; Northwest Area Foundation, and
United Arts. Coffee House also thanks Jeffrey Scherer for a dona-
tion for this book made on behalf of Lea Babcock.

Coffee House Press books are distributed to trade by Consor-
tium Book Sales and Distribution, 287 East Sixth Street, Suite
365, Saint Paul, Minnesota 55101. Our books are also available
through all major library distributors and jobbers, and through
most small press distributors, including Bookpeople, Book-
slinger, Inland, Pacific Pipeline, and Small Press Distribution.
For personal orders, catalogs or other information, write to:
COFFEE HOUSE PRESS
27 NORTH FOURTH STREET, SUITE 400, MINNEAPOLIS, MN 55401.

Library of Congress Cataloging in Publication Data
Greenberg, Alvin.
        Why we live with animals : poems / by Alvin Greenberg.
            p. cm.
        ISBN 0-918273-78-1: $8.95
    1. Animals – Poetry. 2. Sonnets, American. I. Title.
PS3557.R377W48   1990
811'.54 – dc20   90-40518
                        CIP

Second Printing

for

Midge

who first asked this question

and

Sonny

who provided many of the answers

1

the child of your dreams slips into the world wet
and quick, a sudden bundle of teeth and claws
shredding the welcome you've prepared for it,
hairy, rancid, yelping: not at all
the sort of creature you thought you'd get.
the moral's simply this: when the sky falls
you learn to live with fallen sky — and put
your purebred hopes onto whatever pulls
at the long leash of your heart. something will
sniff your socks and lay its head in your lap
as if it were all you ever asked for. perhaps
it is: just feel, when you try to pull
your fingers through that sticky, stinking fur,
how quickly you're entangled with what's here.

2

the uncle who ran away to sea, the cousin
with a steel plate in his head, the frantic
aunt knitting herself tightly into the attic,
grampa's way with spiders and father's obsession
with the struggles of the english over succession
to the throne, to say nothing of mother's quick
successes with the over-the-counter market
and her wayward children and souffles and high fashion
glamorize some other family's life.
in mine, they tell no stories. we eat soup
a lot and pay our bills and that's that.
we think it's good when the rain stops,
and even say so, wife to husband, husband to wife.
mostly what we talk about's the cat.

3

something's on the prowl out there and we
know it. not some half-starved, cellar-
shuffling, chain-clanking wall-knocker
in velvet slippers and smoke. worse. we
feel it flutter beyond the edge of our
fire, tangible as a tornado. it waits:
quiet, hungry, quick, smart, and faster
than the flame that snaps its way, flick of our
hope and bluster. it smells like rotten meat
and howls the high, pure decibels of hate.
its breath's all fangs and claws. it loves the dark.
it can wait forever for us to turn our backs.
oh household pets, we know we ask too much
who keep you to place yourselves between it and us

4

in case of emergency please notify
sonny, who's waiting for me to come home and fix
him his dinner: who's trained me so well to do tricks
—to open doors and fetch him his bones and sigh
when he shits—that surely he'll want to know why
if i don't show up: why and where his next
meal's coming from: and the next and the next . . . .
oh, it's lovely to be missed. to justify
one's comings and goings by another's needs
may be the perfect route to happiness.
lovers and children, the stronger they become,
the more they learn to need one less and less.
but sonny just adores the one who feeds
him: so call to let him know i won't be home.

5

if, when i wake at four a.m., the room's
so thick with dogbreath i can't catch my own
or step from bed without my foot coming down
on a furry back or thigh; if cats bloom
darkly on every sill in every room
and the hallway to the bath is overgrown
with animals; if i think, in the jungly dawn,
that i'm in my own bed and this is my own home,
then i deserve whatever happens here.
this is the world that i invited in;
now i'm inhabited by its devouring will.
it feeds upon my roof, my walls, my air.
the wonder is it sometimes licks my hand.
the peaceable kingdom eludes me still.

6

the howl that reaches from the dog right up
to the stars the moment you leave the house is welcome
news. you pause, your key just above the ignition,
thinking: someone misses me. some pup,
at any rate, would rather have you home
than not. but still, someone's got to shop
for dinner, do the laundry, banking, troop
through the everyday like a good soldier or doom
us all to howl, hungry, behind locked doors
forever. so: since such howling makes a circle of
your absence, put the key in (thank you), turn
the motor on (ah, listen to that purr),
hit the streets and get those errands done.
someone back here's desperate for your love.

7

bird at the feeder, bird on the rail: chickadee,
if you only knew what my life was really like.
call in the purple finch, the evening grosbeak,
the warblers, sparrows, orioles, the phoebe
i've only heard in the distance. listen to me,
lovers, i know what you're doing here. take
that summer sky or the chipmunk under the deck,
the hummingbird battling it out with the bee,
take my raspberries, i know you will: no one's
fooled by all this foolishness, least of all
you tourists. when the time comes, you're south
with everything that matters: feathers, tunes,
tales. except for you, chickadee, like me, pal,
faking it through the winter's seedy truths.

8

all our lives dreamdogs, dreamcats have lived
with us, rising up when we lie down
to prowl the house that we presume to own.
no nightbird sings for them, but they survive
those hours of the absence of our eyes
by sniffing at the hem of the nightgown
you've kicked the covers off or listening to the moan
i make, beside you. the world they improvise
out of the random buzz and clatter of our sleep's
the world we wake to: paw prints on the sills,
fur balls in the corners, echoes of nails
clicking across oak floors, hisses and growls
of the busy demiurge that our dreams keep
up all night licking our days into shape.

9

we walk out to the garden on this spring
morning, the grass wetting our feet and the mutts
leaping and running and peeing, delighted to be out
of the thick bedroom air. the buds are turning
themselves inside out on the apple tree, and green
things in the ground are declaring they, too, want out:
there are better things to do than being shut
up in the dark beneath the garden, and learning
what, they seem to say, is what it's all about:
you can skip the boring details of the lesson
plan nature's figured out for us, we'd love
just to see what we can see all by ourselves:
just look how everything wants out, out, out,
and even the dogs go reasonably crazy in this season.

here's the cat that prefers to drink from the bowl
the dogs use, and here's the bowl those dogs
have emptied once again, and the sink that's clogged
with dog hairs where ten times a day we fill
that bowl, and underneath the sink, the tools
and chemicals we drag out to unplug
our stuffed-up drains, and deeper still the ugly
intricacies of pipe that bring us fresh, cool
water. and here, out here: the dead patches
of grass that show us where the dogs have been:
oh, the bountiful, well-watered grass that teaches
us how to be green, and water's absurdly faulty
notion that the world can sink and rise again
even where it ends up dry and brown and salty.

11

there are things in the air of which we do not speak
but should: we put them there, like heavy furniture,
and in the earth as well. yes, everywhere
we go, we go clawing our way through back
doors into dead cities we thought we'd sneaked
safely away from eons ago. oh sure,
we're dreamers too: who'd think the past could capture
us in such wooden arms? what we've shucked
off, it seems, is sure to have us yet.
i also mean that garbage we call the sea, acid
rain, spoiled soil, soot in your lungs and the knot
in your gut: you ate that. we're not the placid
nomads we thought: no deserts bloom where we were:
what we are curls up at our feet right here.

12

here's this pen that cost a dollar eighty
nine, made for maybe two cents
in taiwan, and i brood about that difference
sometimes—such profit! for someone!—but it's no great
issue in my life, it's just my favorite
pen, not because it represents
the triumph of capitalism, but because the dents
in the cap show where the puppy tried to chew it
up but failed. and maybe that is, in truth,
the achievement of free enterprise: this thing
so well-designed and profitable and proof
against the gnawings of the world (although the pup's
big new teeth show how she's growing up)
and far removed from the misery of its making.

13

mother told me pigs make perfect pets,
playful, sweet, intelligent, and clean,
happy with any scraps, never a mean
thought in their heads. don't, she said, forget
the trouble you've always had with dogs and cats.
so i got one: only a little thing,
fresh from the farm, terrified, just weaned,
a squealer – mother didn't mention that.
i'll grant you, it was plenty smart. it could
conjugate the verb 'to eat' all day
and watched the news before it went to bed
(my bed, that was – while i slept on the floor).
but brains aren't everything. smoked ham's the way
to show someone she should have told me more.

14

the three-inch-high wooden statue my grand-
father carved of michael, the black and white cocker spaniel,
our first dog, sits on my brother's living room table
alongside which his ill-mannered new white poodle stands:
reminders, both, of how the relentless variety of dogs
       hounds
us all our lives. just think of them all!
the ones that are with us still, sonny and lily,
retrievers, yellow, and domino the old dalmatian,
and rosie, wild rosie, the irish setter. and think
of our whole history of dogs: lassie (lassie!), bernard
the saint bernard, beebe brief and black, that great
dane schnapps, dora, dear dora, shiloh and louis and sweet
sad sam—how all the colors and dispositions they've
       shared
with us won't let the world be merely what we think.

15

the man sitting in his living room window
looks at the giant maple flaming out
across the street and thinks, it did that
all by itself. and when it begins to snow
not long after, he thinks, yep, that too,
remembering the tornado that suddenly quit
last june just as it started down his street.
the world, he thinks, will do what it will do
perfectly well on its own, without asking my
permission. for proof, buds and skies burst
open in april while he still sits: just look,
he thinks, at that—ditto how summer burns by.
finally he rises—nearly the end of august!—
choosing (he thinks) to take the dog for a walk.

16

were they too busy to have pets, those jewish
immigrants? why did i have to wait three
generations of dogless citizenry
for my first cocker spaniel? did the irish
or italians wait that long—or bring goldfish,
gerbils, cats, and dogs right with them? see
how, in early paintings, the cherokee
camps are full of dogs, and the colonial english
ride to the hounds, and every settler going
west has a pie-dog trailing behind his horse.
not that peddler, tailor, jeweler, of course.
was keeping cats like living with the goyim?
or were they just waiting for the moment to begin
when they could invite their own immigrants in?

17

how much like you these subatomic bits
i read about dance their dance around
bits more subatomic still, which, found,
will be dancing, doubtless, to the twitch
of still more sub-, sub-, subatomic bit:,
a hidden choreography that grounds
almost every step in mysteries
we can't resolve – and can't forget.
the news on the galactic scale's the same:
the radical speed at which the universe
seems always to have been in flight from us
suggests that things out there are even worse
than here, with us, in the animate wilderness,
dancing the dance no physics can explain.

18

just like the dog that tries to run and pee
at the same time the moment she's let out
and does, instead, a little *danse macabre,*
front end bouncing while she drags her butt,
the mind itself's absurd that tries to grab
for everything at once, when our sole certainty's
that heisenberg won't let us quite forget
the price we pay for what we choose to know.
'if ya gotta go,' i say, 'ya gotta go,'
and your bar stool spins, your ice cubes melt,
watering an absence you don't know . . . yet.
we squirm the worst for what we cannot be,
just like that dog that tries to run and pee
at the same time the moment she's let out.

19

i walk in the roseville pet cemetery where
bobby is urged to perform for the heavenly host
the tricks he did on earth, and ghostly
visits are requested of shadow the cat by mary
and arnold, and 'baby, you were always my very
own, love, moms.' the theme is gratitude, mostly,
and the flowers real, marigolds and asters
from home gardens, but no one else is ever here,
not even a stray dog sniffing the stones.
oh, maybe a squirrel sits up on the wrought-
iron fence, contemplating the surrounding oaks,
and someone trims the grass and someone brought
those flowers, of course, but i'm the one who walks,
dogless and catless, this acre of loyal bones.

20

why is that grown man standing about
at the end of a leash, watching an animal shit?
is that the sort of life he ought to be leading?
shouldn't there, somehow, be something more to it
than standing around on the edge of the park pleading
with a dog to be done with its business without
attracting the attention of the neighbors?
these are serious questions. you've got to admit
that tying yourself to an animal while it shits
in public, hoping, meanwhile, that others will ignore
you, seems a little odd. the poor dog labors
with its back hunched up, while you stand around
        pretending it's
just another lovely day—and that's
in spite of the rain. say, oh say, there's more.

21

set the clock for six a.m.: tomorrow
you'll be up early for once, dressed and ready
for whatever happens, your hand steady
on the wheel as you drive to work. tomorrow
will be a day of shined shoes, the tomorrow
you've always dreamed of, all your bills paid
from a balanced account, your politics worldly
and your oil changed. you'll smile, tomorrow,
ready as never before for nothing at all,
the nothing already headed your way, the nothing
you can't get up early enough for, the nothing
that keeps the cat on the neighbor's roof all
night and the dog howling its hourly howl
and you awake, your eye on the luminous dial.

22

to be reminded, when a summer morning shudders
itself awake and the fog screens off everything
that should be green and greener, that the things
we intended to hang out on the line don't matter
at all, that even the weather doesn't matter,
with the tattered, unseasonable draperies it hangs
out for us to draw conclusions from, nothings
of grey, is to see how we only make things harder
for ourselves with the search for intelligent life
in the universe. maybe it would be different if
the universe flew the flag of an intelligent place.
and maybe it did, just for a moment, once, when the big
bang dotted with spangles of cats and dogs
the sudden stupidity of all that empty space.

23

unlike the way you leave a spoon and a dish
in the sink in cold, greasy water not
because you think someone else should finish
your task or your legs ache or your heart
just isn't in it (though maybe because you wish
you'd won the lottery or some sudden shot
of passion or matter of principle flashes
by like one of those famous detergents that cuts
through anything), but just, well, for lack
of any other way to put it, your undesire
to do it all, it doesn't bother me
when the dog drops the stick halfway back
or slops its water on the kitchen floor.
what a dog is, is all that it can be.

24

trees are such sad pals, that won't come
halfway, and rocks, too: you can sit on
them but only so long. and the garden's
a summer romance. and where you're from
you can't stake too much on the sun's
predictable desertion: when it's done
with you it heads south and you're home
alone like an abandoned lover, a bowl
of polished stones on the coffee table,
a fig tree wilting in its red clay pot,
and a freezer full of your own vegetables.
everything's harder, colder, than it ought
to be. if you could, you'd howl.

2 5

i've been to the woods again and heard the story
of how, if i lived there, i'd be a happier thing,
as told in the voices of animals singing
their traditional tunes of sex and territory.
i've been to the woods again and come back sorry
that i wasn't able to join them in that singing,
had nothing to sing for, only myself to bring
into that subdivided wilderness where i
knew no place, no music, only a little hope.
and though the voices of animals sang again
and again of what was theirs and what they'd share
with me, nothing their singing promised could keep
me there, away from this undivided wilderness where
brushing the dog is such a quieter form of pain.

26

oh my babies, he cries, direct as any
tornado churning its way through this heart-
land: my babies (his voice like a freight
train roaring him down into this tiny
dumbstruck, huddled, southwest basement cranny),
my babies who are here and where, apart
as the roof from the barn: resettled, unhurt,
all grown, just fine: but not here: on these funny
back-of-everything roads he's driving now,
small storms themselves that spin him left and right,
daring him to find a straight way out. he knows
you can't outrun these things, but oh, he tries.
lucky for him, there's a dog in the back seat
making sure the car curves where the road does.

27

when i gave up at last the lifelong search
for the meaning of things – knowing it wasn't to be
found in you, although of course i see
how wonderful you are, and true, which,
probably, the meaning of things is not – to watch,
instead, the things themselves, the *what* that simply
was or happened, and not only to you or me
but the world, the world, in all its every and each,
the first thing i saw was the neighbor's raggedy collie
gobbling the pile of dogshit on our front lawn.
what happens happens, and what is, friends, is.
i clapped my hands and the dog looked up, neither folly
nor glory on its long face. only, finally, this:
when i looked again both dog and dogshit were gone.

28

this substantial ball of fur, the earth,
spins through our lives like something we picked
up at the local toy shop, some gyroscopic
gimmick good, at a party, for an easy laugh
when the cosmic wind takes it in its teeth
or when it shakes and bristles at the tracks
we finger along its back. sure, it's comic,
but armatured, like any toy, with truth,
it turns and turns like some huge, wary beast
bedding down uneasily in our midst,
closing its eyes but never really asleep.
the light dims. its coat's rough landscape
softens. for the moment we feel safe: lost
children dreaming oceans, mountains, forests.

29

what the computer has to say is that we
should love one another, but it
doesn't believe a word of that: it's
just information, of a sort. we
should, of course: the consequences we
know, even without all the data it
projects: tables, graphs, stats: its
way of loving us—but only because we
told it to. but the love we ordered's not
the one we want. something we didn't quite
deserve or even ask for's what we'd like
to see come crawling off that screen one night,
something that's nothing *we* could have thought,
something that growls or purrs for its own sake.

30

the old dog enters the water as if it were
his home, paddling around in circles, head up
and happy, while the other, still half pup,
paws the shallows, all splash and splatter
at the edge, making her own toy out of a river
that, a hundred yards downstream, drops
thirty deadly feet off the mill dam's lip
to the chaos of broken rock and broken water.
it's summer now. the river's low and mild
that might, in flood, pluck even a good-sized
dog off its banks and sweep it swiftly away.
but it's summer now, and we are not surprised
by anything water does: by anything wilder
than one dog swimming and another one at play.

31

there are more ways to go than animals, every
one of them a dilemma. the straight line
is ours, leaving other creatures behind
as if they were burdens we weren't sorry
to drop by the side of the road. but the history
of dogs keeps circling us, now downwind,
now laying a scent so dense even we can find
what we live in the midst of. and the history
of cats is like the very floor we walk on,
all tongue and groove. and the vertical history
of birds and fish plunges through our dreams –
while our own stays straight and thin: an old story:
the intricate knot, the emperor's sudden weapon,
the way ahead as long and empty as it seems.

32

two blocks straight ahead and one block right
will take you home again: decades back
into the soft, enormous arms your folks
even then could never hold you tight
enough with. one block more, just out of sight
of home, your first childhood love still lurks,
shy and bony as ever, with a promise that seeks
you out even now on sweaty summer nights.
above this neighborhood the succulent domes
and towers of your schools arise, cumulative
as clouds; and office buildings you once were sure
were solid steel and stone are just another sieve
you sift through, groping for the hold of home.
there's nothing left to fall into but fur.

33

all the season's holidays are past:
memorial day, midsummer night, the fourth;
wimbeldon's over, and, for what it's worth,
the all-star game's been played. congress has passed
its final bills and an august heat wave's chased
everyone off the streets. even the faith
we had last spring that we remembered the path
through the dunes to the beach is as inexplicably lost
as the summer itself: that flurry of fireworks
and the total darkness after in which no one
could find anyone's hand to hold, and the dog gone
somewhere loose in the crowd, and everyone
crying out 'come, dog, come,' and the fiery weeks
still advancing on autumn in their sweaty uniforms.

34

we are that stuffed cat that guards the hats
in the london haberdasher's window where
you stood five rainy minutes trying to decipher
us. well, we're alive, always alive because that's
what you need us to be, windowsful of exhibits
at the natural history museum, bison, saber-
toothed tiger ready to spring, even poor trigger
in roy roger's living room. you think it's
easy, you who were there at the cincinnati zoo
when the earth's last passenger pigeon bought it?
duty, that's what: your own dead you can fling
into the earth, but we always have to be with you:
that small pile of bones in the back of the closet
or out of the melting glacier, the unnameable *thing*.

35

you and i, dear, in our separate cages hang
from spruce limbs where the bears can't get us,
but whose dinner are we then? even in august
the fog on its famous feet creeps up the ravine
with just a touch of ice in its whiskers. nothing
to be done: the tigers have slipped loose
from their stripes and are orangely playing house
in our backyard. but before the year is lean
and cool again, summer's still got six
full weeks of fat to sweat away. who said
anything about malice? this didn't happen just
because, like yeats, we, too, were 'once afraid
of turning out reasonable.' did it? these leaks
in the roof of the world? this picnic? all the rest?

36

the hand trembles: if there were no animals
to slide their heads up under it for soothing,
it would tremble worse. how quiet it is, smoothing
the fur down on the big dog's head. animals
ease us like water: the tide of great animals
rising in the night sky, an evening of falling
wings splashing into birches, the cat flowing
across your chest when you lie back: animals,
always waiting for us to wade among them: oceans
of animals: in the streets, the skies, the woods,
in zoos, at home, right down in the backyard grass,
the warm, shallow oceans of the beginnings of worlds,
magenta, salt, reptilian, oceans of absolution,
the same turgid oceans we slithered out of once.

37

born into a house with only a mother and father,
how did you survive? where did you turn
when you turned from the breast? how did you learn
to sniff the night air while your parents gathered
together books and friends in nearby rooms. either
some furred and clawed invisible sibling was born
beside you or you worked some infant charm
on that herd of button-eyed beasts they tried to smother
you under, sniffing a hiss or a snarl out of anything
close. no, no one dares to come into this world
alone. better to be raised by wolves than to dream
that people are enough. where's the dimension of doing
when a world spawning in its own dark ponds is ignored?
if animals didn't exist, we'd have to invent them.

38

winter again—almost—and the foolish yellow
dog steps out onto the barely frozen lake,
his trust in the thin crust of snow. one bark
from old apathy here and i, fool, follow
wind-blown paw prints through snow shallows
over the depths the glacier left, unshaken
by how, with every shift the ice makes,
the lake booms and echoes in its hollow
bowl of hills. i close my eyes and call
this limbo lake. i know what lies below.
i know the frozen waters will not part
for my sake. ice: ice to the very heart.
and i know the yellow dog will slowly circle
out, then back, to see if we can, now, go.

39

and then there are some places it doesn't help
to have an animal with you, so i shut
the dog in the car in the church parking lot
and walk across the cemetery all by myself,
my shoes filling with snow, my coat half
open so i can feel what it's like out
here, my hands lost in my pockets, my hat
tight in the wind, and, as usual, no scarf.
oaktree. snowdrift. cloudlight. windsong.
the world has left its signature in stone.
there are no other footprints but my own,
coming in, then trailing out to where the dog,
sitting, as he loves to, in the driver's seat,
reminds me that there's more to this than grief.

4 0

to know, finally, nothing: a refuge everyone
should huddle in from time to time, nose
in the carpet, nose in the feedbag. whose
turn to understand? i dunno. someone
else's. snout in the mud, i say: anyone
can know, will do. for now, this: to choose
just to lie at the foot of something: sighs
of ignorance: ahhh, nothing, ahhh, no one.
nostalgia? yes. in the beginning this pure
silence between the ears: all nose, eyes,
teeth, and claws: thing-things and the tools
for assembling a world where nightly we'd curl
up on the rug by the fire of our own surprise,
free from this racket of knowledgeable fools.

41

the only sign of life in the house is a note
on the kitchen table, saying, oh, please feed
the canary (what canary?) and if the dog needs
a walk (there's no dog) please take him out
and change the litterbox (no, there's no cat
either) because even imagined animals have needs
and mine is just to think that someone reads
this meaningless note even if no one wrote it.
just think, then: someone reads it, filled
with grief and confusion and a sudden urge
to open cupboards. well, no mouse turds
in the sink, no spider webs, but in the still
kitchen something scrapes the air, the floor:
something that wasn't in the house before.

42

no then, no one home, no one, not a
girl or a boy, not an old granddad, a belch,
a whisper, a puff of smoke, not the crash
of a tear in the aunt's room, no, not a
whimper, raising those kids by herself, not a
sigh by the hall telephone, not the flash
of pop's gold money clip or the steady twitch
in the kid's left eye, nothing, no one, not a
dream, lord no, the dreams are all long gone.
got off the leash in the park one day and never
returned. dreams have a life of their own
and can make it, maybe, in the wild, alone.
not us. nope. only when they choose to live
with us is there, finally, anybody home.

43

sit. speak. fetch. down. stay.
i am wearied with instruction: the ball
always finding its way back, full
of saliva and devotion, the need to say
a few more significant words, the need to play
chase games in the yard, to take us all
for a ride in the car, to fill the water bowl.
what i really need's to get away
for a little while. this learning's rough:
so much to remember, so much they ask us
simply to take on faith. i'm just a man
trying to do his best, to study, practice,
but the hours are long and the teacher's tough:
for now i think i've learned about all i can.

4 4

some days even the grass shouts
how you're not welcome: get away! get off!
the trees spit on you and the house has had enough
of you, too: the moment you left, it locked you out.
and one look at the sky's all it takes to find out
there's no place for you there. you'd stuff
yourself in a hole in the ground just to be safe
for an hour somewhere where there's nothing else about,
but the rocks, the rocks! and the shovels have all left town
and those clouds: the rain's sure to wash you loose
before you've taken even one deep breath
of dirt. and forget the river—it's got no use
for your lonely bones, for a life looped around
an empty leash. you don't even interest death.

4 5

took old sonny into a bar one time
and he was good, i mean he just laid
down on the floor beside my stool and stayed
there, while this guy on the stool next to mine
stared and stared, then wanted to know what kind
of dog that was. a yellow lab, i said,
and he said, no, it ain't, and i was afraid
for a minute there that suddenly i'd find
myself entangled in some stupid barroom brawl
for the first time in my life, battered, bloody,
down on my knees on the floor – and all for a dog.
life, friends, is difficult. and that's not all:
you're always coming up against some moody
son-of-a-bitch looking for someone to slug,

46

but i didn't give an inch: he's a yellow lab,
i said (because he is), and this old guy
drained his beer and looked me in the eye
and said, again, he ain't. friends, i'm misled
by so many things that i've just got to grab
at the rare, pure, simple truth that comes my way.
now i don't like to see blood shed, especially my
own, but dammit, a yellow lab's a yellow lab,
even if mixed, a little, with golden retriever,
and so after a little pause i said, yes, he is,
and drank my beer and waited to eat my teeth.
but he just paid and left. friends, did you ever
know truth to have such a moral bark as this?
speak, always speak up: a dog's an act of belief.

47

life inside a tornado's not any life
at all. talk about things flying around,
it's words, words, words, up and down
the stairs, down on your knees in the teeth
of your expectations, and they take your breath
away: i've read in the paper how they found
a straw blown through a fence post. that wind
spears me down cellar steps: nothing safe,
and as for the long tradition of false
weather reports, i don't even want to know why,
i've had it with people and how they explain
their unpredictable storms. as the man said, 'i
think that i could turn and live with animals,
they are so placid and self contain'd.'

48

how far would the world have ever gotten past
us, past me and you if it hadn't been for them?
nowhere: nothing could ever have been the same
if it weren't for the white-tailed deer, for the least
of the warblers, even the coyote, that pest,
or the armadillo, leaping, surprised, into your arms.
i'm not just talking about what we've managed to tame,
but every unlikely, unloved, indelicate beast
that intrigues or eludes us, scratches, slithers, nests
in the eaves, mates in the air or the sea without shame,
reminds us, with its teeth, that we, too, are food.
what would be here if they weren't? silence is the best
we'd manage without them: yes, without them, what would
we say? in all that quiet, what would we have to name?

4 9

prescription: dog: take one three times a day
for a walk in the park. take four. take five
or six. take whatever it takes to keep you alive
and out of trouble. leash up the cat on your way
out the door. the gerbil. the parrot. and hey!
don't forget the tropical fish: they can save
your life as quick as the rabbit, which you can shove
under your jacket while stowing the white mice away
in your pockets. with the hamster under your hat
and the duck tucked under your arm, you're all set
for the worst the world can do, ready to go forth
with all the protection you need. why, no one can see
if there's even anyone there: just a mobile menagerie
strolling the park, the very picture of health.

50

there's only one serious question, and this
is it: why do we live with animals
with all those people waiting to be our pals,
to join the family, bring us a little bliss
or a little woe or make some zany sacrifice
on our behalf, feed us, clean us, fill
our plates and glasses, fill our hearts, all
those colleagues, lovers, friends, foes,
standing on the front lawn, wanting in?
crowds everywhere, and yet that's not
quite enough. too much, perhaps: but still
something's missing: something to part
that mob, saying, who're you? something
that isn't us: some other animal.

51

if, from the concept of animals you take
the simple idea of dog, and then refine
that further still—say you have in mind
some regulation breed, whose image you make
out of color and coat, height, nose, bark,
bite, ears and tail and appetite—define
it however you want—then set out to find,
in pet shop or pound, some critter like
you've thought up, what do you think you'll get?
daily the sun comes up on a different world.
even the face in the mirror's changed—a bit.
everywhere around you the particulars lie curled
in their corners, anything but asleep:
one of them waits for the one of you it'll keep.

52

well, yes, ok, then, but why these particular
pets? cats, sure. dogs, you bet. a parakeet,
a gerbil, the occasional turtle, perhaps. but
the details arrive like a demented trucker
running the light: you never bargained for
an oversized cat that loves to paw your tits
or this gangly pooch with her teenager's feet
and hopes. nothing demanded that. either
the world's got your number, you think, and no
one obeys the laws when you're around, or, worse,
there are no laws, you never had a prayer,
the world's a traffic accident, you're there.
but not just any you. the universal curse
is that particularity is all there is. and so.

53

there's four walls here you can bounce off of
until you're tired of them, then you can try
the other rooms: four more, four more: sanctify
yourself with bruises as if that'll prove
your prayers are answered because the sky's caved
in on all the limbs you've tendered, the ivy
battered in the hanging baskets: passivity
everywhere, waiting for you to shove
it aside just as fast as you hauled it in.
but just because greenery puts up with your fuss
doesn't make it right. fish, flesh, and fowl
might look on your act with the snap and scowl
you save for yourself: they're animals, pal, and
as one of the famous ones says, they're us.

54

the dog lies on the rug in a patch of sun
like nobody could, and the kitten demonstrates she
can do it just as well. competency
comes our way like that sometimes, like a run
of cloudless days, cheap and easy, but un-
predicable. tomorrow it rains and we
back into the neighbor's car just as naturally
as we ever breathed. this, friends, is not fun,
and we'd like to think that somewhere, somewhere solace
shines and, just this once, in the ninth,
two out, two on, and two strikes down, he'll hit
one out. we want so much from a little sunshine.
later, however, we watch a guy frying greasy
burgers, and we know a cat can't do that.

55

whatever you let in the house can eat you up,
you know. you open the door, the wind comes in
and cleans you out, just like that, not even
a stick of furniture left that won't cut
your heart out with a rusty spring, bed slat's
snap breaking you in half, all comfort gone
and hospitality nothing but a myth when even
the fish can nibble you to death, guppies
as well as piranha, and you know it for sure
when you wake in the blue-lit night and listen,
lying there, to the fish tank, breathing.
sounds like you might as well stuff your own hand
down the disposal, where the rats are waiting,
but first, let's consider what you had before:

56

ok, that was easy enough and quick: therefore,
being, like all men, mortal, and, moreover,
having your myths as well as your solitudes,
you invited, from time to time, friends over
for drinks and your hot cuisine, the short tour
of what you thought you had: your art, your moods.
so there was clearly plenty of room for guests
and you invoked the myth of hospitality,
nothing to fear from them, from you: see
if the rules are right: choose to toast
the enemy, sleep with both eyes closed, trust
her with the crystal: choose, for once, not to be
fearful of waking in the middle of the night to pee
and finding something with claws inside your chest

57

though whatever you let in the house can eat you
up, and you might have been better off to have
started small and without trying to save
everything from teeth and claws. the gods who
come to your door with ratty coats and—wheeoo!
a stench like that—are a lesson in how to behave
like your parents never taught you: believe,
if not in them, then in the slice of meat you
carve, for their first meal, from your own heart.
hospitality's the art of sacrifice.
what the puppy did to the couch is no guarantee
that good's gonna come your way. the rug may be
the next to go. but still, this dog, that cat,
offer what you most need: a chance to practice

58

with loss, with the endless nibbling away,
with this: *morturari te salutamus*
by letting those animals who will befriend us.
tornados, after all, don't know how to play
and fire wants to have everything its way;
dirt's a passively hostile, insidious guest
and water's always rushing to be somewhere else:
like the government, the elements say
you can't live without them, then a mudslide
devours you without your ever inviting it home.
such determined anthromorphs! sure,
you always take your chances: what you decide
to let in the house *can* eat you up: but you're
the one to choose just what will gnaw your bones.

59

when the dog comes home with a deer leg in his mouth,
wagging his tail and ducking his head to show
how happy he is with his prize although he knows
you'll disapprove, and you see that delicate hoof
between his jaws, the whole thing terribly uncouth,
tattered and dry, long dead, but he won't let go
and even growls a little at your grab, your "no!"
—you know you're caught in the teeth of a larger truth
than you ever expected when you brought that puppy home.
something's gnawing at the fine veneer you've laid
like the decent pet owner you are over both your table
manners: your dish, his bowl, so it was once agreed.
now it's not that your companion's grown less
            companionable
but that something in you, too, hungers for the bone.

6 0

the air is eaten up by sunlight and the clean snow
devours the sunlight and even though it's january
there's a green threat to the morning and surely no one, no
one, can chart a path through such a forest of glare
and glitter: because we cannot live alone with what we know
or when the ignorance of spring breaks through marry
the answer to absence of ice, because i love you
and any temperature above the freezing mark worries
me more than the arrival of the burpee seed catalogue
with its nightmarish blue potatoes and hundred pound
       squash,
because out of its contrast with the zero air it's not
the lake, tomorrow, will wave its curtain of fog
at us like the ultimate insult: because of all of that, what
we live with eats and breathes and moves and isn't us.